New York
in the 1930s

Samuel Fuller

New York
in the 1930s

POCKET 🦢 ARCHIVES

HAZAN

ARCHIVE PHOTOS ™

All of the photographs contained in the present work
are from the collection of Archive Photos in Manhattan,
with the exception of those appearing on pages 12-13
and 39, which are from the author's collection.

Cover illustration: Central Park

© Éditions Hazan, Paris, 1997
Editor: Éric Reinhardt
Design: Atalante
Production: Anouk Garin and Maya Masson
Color separation: Seleoffset, Torino
Printing: Milanostampa, Farigliano

ISBN: 2 85025 534 3
Printed and bound in Italy

Contents

According to the writer Gene Fowler - whom I have always considered as my mentor since my early days as a copy boy in Manhattan – the expression "Nevertheless" perfectly describes the atmosphere of New York in the Roaring Twenties. As Gene wrote in his novel, *Skyline*: "It was a world of *nevertheless*, a rosy time, the complexion of which now has faded like a clown's face in the rain." These were also the "dry" years of Prohibition, marked by brutality and organized crime. When the twenties had finally roared themselves out, America found itself in the hard years of the Depression, during which Manhattan seemed like an island of fabricated artifice with a paradoxical predilection for the natural and the primitive.
In 1927, the American public, already divided into two hostile camps by the execution of Sacco and Vanzetti,

became passionately involved in still another drama: those who felt that Ruth Snyder should be executed in the electric chair, and those who felt that she should escape the death penalty. And as with Sacco and Vanzetti, it was the first camp that won. Ruth was thirty-three when she was strapped into the chair for the murder of her forty-six-year-old husband. During the interval between her trial and execution, she attained celebrity status as a martyr to the cause of women's rights with the feminists of the late twenties and early thirties. But in the end, and despite an impassioned defence plea, all that she got for her fame was the Murder-One verdict demanded by the State of New York and a headline-epitaph from the sensationalist press: "She Killed Her Husband Because She Loved Another Man." Ruth Snyder served as the inspiration for James M. Cain's novel, *The Postman Always Rings Twice* and the three films that were adapted from the book. During her trial, she received twenty-five hundred letters of sympathy from women who approved of her homicidal revolt against the husband she hated. There were also poignant notes from her nine-year-old daughter, who was praying for her acquittal. The writer Damon Runyon, the philosopher Will Durant, sob-sister columnist Peggy Hopkins Joyce of the *New York Daily Mirror* and the Jesus con-man Reverend Billy Sunday were among those covering the trial known as "the great murder circus." This Wagnerian real-life opera was in perfect harmony with the spirit of the times – and of Manhattan itself in 1928 – as it swept men and women away in a whirlwind of scandal and hysteria. While waiting for her last walk down Death Row, Ruth received nearly two hundred offers of marriage. My friend Gene Fowler covered the execution for *The New York American*: when it was over, the body of Ruth's lover Judd Gray was wheeled through the dark corridors to the prison morgue and placed on the stone slab next to hers. That evening, atop *The New York Times* building on Times Square, the first banner headline on the first electric news sign in America announced: RUTH SNYDER... ELECTROCUTED... IN CHAIR.... On the radio, the latest hit song was called *Crazy Rhythm*.

The first execution by electricity, an experiment performed on a ten-pound turkey in 1773, led to the electrocution of Ruth Snyder in 1928. On Friday January 13, the entire front page of the *New York Daily News* was devoted to a photograph of Ruth – taken by a hidden camera – in the electric chair the instant before her execution. The photo, which equally shocked New Yorkers and the American public, provoked a national debate on capital punishment. The barometer of a turbulent America from 1914 to 1928, the passion and tragedy of her life marked not only the thirties, but still exercises the same fascination on people today.

* * *

I was raised in Manhattan, one of the most frenetic cities in the United States, and still one of my favorites. Most of my memories come from the unforgettable moments I have spent there: I have a deep love and respect for the place, the indescribable feeling that one has when one's love is profound. My dream was to become a reporter: New York made my dream come true and made me what I am today. Lower Manhattan was the area I preferred, simply because with the exception of *The New York Times*, which was located uptown, all the biggest newspapers had their offices there. I remember how after school, I would hitch a ride on a truck that would drive me all the way downtown to a magical street called Park Row. I rendered homage to it in the early fifties in my film *Park Row*, with Gene Evans and Mary Welsh. Gene was also in my film *The Steel Helmet*; Mary was a Broadway actress for whom Eugene O'Neill had written many of his great plays; she died tragically in childbirth just after we finished the film. I would go to Park Row along with other newsboys to fetch a bundle of newspapers to sell in different parts of town. Since I could only carry a certain quantity, I would have to make several trips back and forth. I remember standing in the middle of the Brooklyn Bridge, where I would dream of the island of Manhattan and the world beyond, experiencing cosmic empathy for the entire universe. Other great bridges spanned the city's rivers: the George Washington Bridge, the Williamsburg and the Manhattan Bridge. Compared to the rest of New York, Manhattan is a small island, but to my nineteen-year-old eyes it seemed the biggest city in the world.

In the beginning, I worked for *The Evening Journal*. This paper gave me a lot of wonderful moments, and I am still grateful to them for letting me start as a copy boy at such a young age. A few months later, I was introduced to the composing room and then to the editorial department. *The Evening Journal* was an important newspaper and very impressive: their headlines were the biggest in New York! Tom Folly, the press foreman, told me that once upon a time the pressroom, which was housed in an incredibly old building, had served as a prison for British troops during the War of Independence. Pressrooms had a great deal of importance for America: history was being made thanks to newspapers, but no one would have been able to read about it had it not been for the great presses and the men who made them run. Their vibrations would penetrate my body; it was a feeling that I will never forget and that will never leave me.

* * *

My father died when I was eleven years old. I was lucky to find work that paid twelve dollars and fifty cents a week before I was even twelve, followed by a job as a copy boy at *The New York Journal* for fifteen dollars. My wages were increased to twenty-five and then to fifty dollars a week when I was only seventeen years old. This was right in the middle of the Depression. I spent very little money on myself, giving most of it to my mother, who was raising seven children while pursuing a friendship with the surrealist poet Max Bodenheim and his eccentric friends. I was happy to see Bodenheim mentioned in Warren Beatty's period film *Reds*; I referred to him as "Dr. Bodenheim" in my film, *Shock Corridor*.

Samuel Fuller copy-boy, *The New York Journal*, 1929

Emil Gavreau, the editor of *The Graphic*, which was the finest paper I have ever known, made me a police reporter when I was barely eighteen years old. The history of *The Graphic* is told in an excellent book entitled *Sauce for the Gander*, whose characters include Emil, Walter Winchel, Ed Sullivan, Mark Hellinger, Jerry Wald, John Huston and myself, among others who were to become famous over the next decades. Emil Gavreau was a hot-shot editor from Connecticut, where he had worked for the *Hartford Courier* until being hired by the multi-millionaire publisher MacFadden. MacFadden had long hair and seven children, all girls. He also liked the cartoons I was doing at the time, and published a dozen or so at twenty-five dollars each.

* * *

Manhattan may have had bread lines during the Depression years, but it rivalled Paris when it came to restaurants, good times and entertainment in general. Above all, there were the nightclubs on upper Broadway, where you could hear groups like the Chuck Webb Band, Benny Goodman and his musicians, and a skinny newcomer named Frank Sinatra. There was The Big Apple, a Harlem nightclub on Seventh Avenue where Billie Holliday sang in 1936, and of course the famous Cotton-Club. Black artists were increasingly instrumental in setting new trends in entertainment. These were the Harlem years of Louis Armstrong, Ethel Waters and Duke Ellington. Black Harlem created a whole new industry out of entertainment that catered mainly to the white population of Manhattan. The atmosphere of Harlem was like ancient Rome; it was a neighborhood that lived by night, and was reputed to have over one hundred nightclubs. Acceleration, speed and velocity were the key words, as blacks and whites packed the clubs to swing to the music of artists like Lionel Hampton, Cab Caloway, "Satchmo" Armstrong and Ella Fitzgerald, just to name a few. It was no longer a question of white entertainers in blackface; we now had the real thing. Blacks were setting the trend for a new and more authentic form of entertainment, even as they tried to overcome racial barriers through rhythm, music, and dance.

My family lived on 125th Street and Broadway in a tenement apartment just a few blocks away from Harlem. In the thirties, the one-dimensional stereotype of blacks began to disappear; part of the Manhattan *Zeitgeist* of this period was the desire for a more truthful understanding of black and white relationships. It was a quest for origins that had started with the Harlem Renaissance of the twenties, in reaction to a world in which Wall Street seemed to rule everything and everyone. The blacks were fighting this kind of alienation; both races tried to understand each other through art, and the most accessible art forms of the period were music, theater and the movies. Radio also became a popular form of communication. Benny Goodman was instrumental in making a star out of Billie Holliday, yet in the Waldorf Astoria she still had to use the service elevator! Being a black singer in a white band had ensured her stardom, but the discrimination was still there. Others, like Josephine Baker, simply chose to leave the country for places like France. And in the meantime in Europe, Hitler's racist propaganda was contaminating the malleable, uneducated and blind masses, infecting the Continent with Nazi hysteria and the death-wish of destruction and genocide. Manhattan became the nocturnal playground for people who began the evening with a Broadway show and then went on to swing all night in Harlem—where one always went in the company of a pretty lady! The Cotton Club, re-created in Francis Ford Coppola's film in the '80s, was in the area along 133rd Street between Lenox and Seventh Avenue known as "Jungle Alley." But places like Connie's Inn, with its Tree of Hopein front of the club that was supposed to bring good luck when you touched it, were just as popular. The interior of Connie's was pitch-black. The clients, mostly chic and white, came to hear black singers and the famous Fletcher Henderson Band. If Connie's clients were generally white, the Catagonia Club was basically black, less chic, but more into authentic Harlem-style fun. Bill Robinson tap-danced there, and the beautiful and magnetic Ethel Waters was also a regular, having begun her career in Harlem's night-spots in the twenties until achieving national success as a singer and actress. Her life is documented in the autobiography *His Eye Is on the Sparrow*, published in the early fifties. Ethel Waters' most popular song was W.C. Handy's *St. Louis Blues* and the 1932 recording of *I Can't Give You Anything but Love*. Her way of singing the blues and pop-jazz was extremely sophisticated, and contributed to the dignity of black culture and the emancipation of black women from white America's oppressive legacy of racism and slavery. She openly rejected the stereotype of black performers, and insisted on her creative and personal independence. By 1933, with a weekly salary of one thousand dollars, she was the best-paid performer on Broadway. Irving Berlin wrote the song *Summertime* especially for her; rebellious and proud, she was the Angela Davies of the twenties and thirties.

If the Cotton Club's reputation has survived so brilliantly up to the present, it was largely because it was such a popular place among artists, writers, foreign visitors and the generally hip: it was a truly cosmopolitan place. But there were a number of other Harlem clubs that were just as much fun, such as The Kentucky Club, where Duke Ellington and his band performed, and The Clam House, whose mainly white clientele had the reputation of being among the most promiscuous of Jungle Alley. There was also the famous Last Stop, with its mixed black-and-white crowd, The Lenox Club, which claimed to have the loudest and hottest band in all of Harlem, and Tillie's Inn, which had a reputation for great food and clients ranging from upper-crust whites from Sutton Place to neighborhood folks from Lenox. Tillie's was also known for its affordable prices and the absence of a cover-charge. The Saratoga Club had a mostly black clientele, and a rule stipulating that one could only dance with one's escort! The Nest Club had a very coy, warm atmosphere, good music, and was one of the most popular Harlem night-spots. The Spider Web had a mostly black crowd and a great band, whereas Small's Paradise was mixed, and had a huge dance floor. The Smoke Shack offered singing waiters and reasonable prices; it was a place where people could dance all night after having enjoyed sandwiches and coffee at the Cotton Coffee Pot, just across the street from the swankier Cotton Club.

* * *

Like a Baudelerian poem, Manhattan always embraces the highs and the lows of existence. In 1929, following a complaint by the Daughters of the American Revolution, Margaret Sanger's birth control clinic was raided by the police, and the doctors and nurses arrested. The charges were ultimately dropped as obstructing the freedom of medical practice, but seventy years later the same incidents have occurred in various parts of the United States, proving once again that *"plus ça change, plus c'est la même chose."*

I also remember the thirties for the bootlegged editions of James Joyce's *Ulysses* which were being smuggled into the country, provoking hysterical reactions against its "obscenity." But in general, people were tired of the past and were yearning for something new. "The Moderns" portrayed in Alan Rudolph's film of the period were determined not to be another "lost" generation like Sylvia Beach and the other Paris exiles of the twenties. Nevertheless, the seduction of European culture was still present, despite modern Manhattan's break with the Old World. At the moment that Anton Tchekov's play *The*

Seagull was enjoying a hit run, one Manhattan cartoonist couldn't resist the ironic caption: "Why should I dress up just to see a play about a bird?" The sublime and the ridiculous are two sides of the same coin in Manhattan, and it's better not to take things too seriously.

* * *

In the same vein, Clarence Day's satirical poems mocked everyone from Adam and Eve to Lancelot and King Arthur. I remember the short poem which accompanied one of his cartoons: "Here's Tristan on the ocean floor being brought up with a jerk—he's discovered that his magic potion doesn't work!" Lampoons such as these attempted to ridicule Old World myths and superstitions, but at the same time, Manhattan was always ready to imitate European values and culture. There were French restaurants galore, such as The Marigny, Longchamps, The Mirlton, The Meadowbrook, The Beau Rivage and The Madisson. But the most popular and famous of all was La Rue's on 480 Park Avenue. The food was so good —and the prices so high—that I couldn't afford to eat there all through the thirties. I compensated for this in the fifties and spent a great deal of money there, making up for lost time. Back in the thirties, La Rue's chef was a man called Peter, famous for his "Cerises Jubilee" and specialities like venison with choucroute. In 1935, New Yorkers were saddened by the disappearance of Mori's Restaurant on 144 Bleeker Street. Founded in 1884 by Placido Mori and decorated by Raymond Hood, it had achieved landmark status by 1913. People came just to marvel over the elegance of its facade, so different from the naked iron girders of the Sixth Avenue, El, just a few blocks away. It was immortalized by the photographer Berenice Abbott, who also did a series of pictures of homeless people living on the waterfront of Manhattan's East River in the late thirties. Many of these dispossessed individuals ended up trying to drown themselves in desperation; today Abbott's prophetic and visionary images are a sad reminder of the homeless populations in the big cities of our industrialized world.

The Longchamps restaurant was frequented by the rich and the famous, as was the German restaurant Luchow's on 110 East 14th Street. Luchow's, with a history that went back to the turn of the century, was a Manhattan classic and still very much in style in the thirties.

Middle-Eastern cuisine was also available, and in the Syrian district one could find baklava, halva, shish-ke-bab and stuffed grape leaves. In the Lebanon Restaurant on 88 Washington Street, I would sip demi-tasses of Turkish coffee while dreaming of ancient cultures and forgotten cities. Manhattan was indeed the most cosmopolitan metropolis in the world—an authentic melting-pot—but still a place where you could satisfy basic Yankee tastes, such as having a good glass of ale in a noisy chop house or a great American-style meal in one of Manhattan's famous grill-rooms. Beef-Steak Charlie's, on 216 West 50th Street, was one of my very favorites as well as my fellow-newspapermen's, despite its noise, overall chaos and come-as-you-are atmosphere.

The gargantuan steaks with onions were just as appealing as the inexpensive bills for working stiffs like us. Oriental and Russian restaurants were also very much in style, mostly on the Lower East Side for the former and in mid-town for the latter. Good Chinese cuisine could be found at the Royal Chinese Grill on Broadway and 71st Street, which also featured a jazz band. The atmosphere of wooden trimmings and pale lights along with a variety of dishes was in demand from Brooklyn to Yonkers and all over Manhattan. There was the Palais d'Or on Broadway and the Peking Garden and Chinaland on Seventh Avenue, just to name a few. The Oriental on Pell Street was the most famous: like the Royal Chinese Grill it also featured a jazz band. As for the rich and the famous, they paid sky-high prices to dine at Dinty Moore's on 216 West 46th Street.

* * *

Manhattan is and was a city of taxis, and cabs were always available to take you to the vaudeville and movie houses, billiard halls, dance palaces and the numerous speak-easies, ranging from the sleazy to the deluxe. The speak-easies existed in the hundreds, and some were venerable institutions. I entered my first speak-easy when I was only fifteen, accompanied by three older reporters: Ring Lardner, Gene Fowler and Bill Farnsworth. Lardner died in 1933; his son Ring Lardner Jr. was a famous screenwriter and one of the Hollywood Ten. Fowler is one of the sources of inspiration for this book; his son Gene Fowler Jr. became my film editor and good friend. Gene Jr.'s wife Marjorie is the daughter of Nunnally Johnson, who wrote the screenplay for the *Grapes of Wrath*. As for Bill Farnsworth, he was simply an all-around great guy and good friend. The speak-easy they took me to was a fairly ritzy place which refused to serve me hard liquor: they probably didn't like having a visibly wet-behind-the-ears kid like myself among their clientele of confirmed, affluent boozers! The owner of the place was Lew Walters, whose daughter was Barbara Walters. Liquor or no liquor, I was still glad to be there sipping up seltzer water through a straw while my elders were knocking back rye whiskies and clouding the air with cigar smoke. There were also a lot of pretty ladies around, most of whom were on the dancefloor entertaining their customers for the evening. Everything seemed terribly adult, marvellously exciting and extremely expensive to my fifteen-year-old eyes. These were still the Depression and Prohibition years, and the Manhattan speak-easies were big businesses which provided physical and spiritual consolation far into the night. The layout was generally invariable: a bar, spittoons and tables; some had back rooms for more privacy and all had tough bouncers for tipsy or aggressive customers who "got out of line."

Some speak-easies offered musical entertainment, but the main attraction—and the reason for their existence—was alcohol. If Paris had attracted such a large expatriate community, surely one of the reasons was that you could still drink legally there. In America, the twenties and thirties were "dry" until Roosevelt was elected president and finally repealed Prohibition.

All kinds of people owned the speak-easies, and one was only admitted through the introduction of a "member." In the case of Lew Walters' place, this was usually a re-porter, a publisher, a stockbroker, a bootlegger or even —like in a *roman noir*—a detective or a beautiful blonde. There were tall mirrors and paintings of nude women on the walls, and a dollar changed hands faster than the eye could see! Even if some speak-easies were classier than others, the tips always had to be generous if you wanted to be welcomed back a second time.

* * *

In the middle of all this fun, dark clouds were piling up on the European horizon. Some representative headlines from *The New York Times*, "published daily including Sundays, and recording world history since 1851": the November 30, 1929 edition reports Byrd's flight to the South Pole and back, and the shooting of casino tycoon Rothstein on the same day. September 19, 1931: the Japanese seize Mukden after fighting the Chinese. November 9, 1932: Roosevelt wins in a landslide, with the Democrats carrying forty states. Tuesday, January 31, 1933: Adolph Hitler becomes Chancellor of Germany; the communists call for a general strike. In France, there are plans for moderate government, but Daladier is unable to get enough support from the socialists; Hitler becomes an issue and budget-cuts are demanded by the French Left, but rejected despite the bad news from Berlin. March 4, 1933: Hitler's rise to power begins to alarm the rest of

Europe. In the United States, Roosevelt calls for an embargo on gold, while hoarders are threatened with prison. Saturday, June 17, 1933: Roosevelt organizes a national recovery program and signs legislation for banks, railroads and industry. Wheat farmers received one hundred million dollars in government subsidies. The Reich demands the return of African territories at a London conference, while casting a hungry eye upon its neighbors in Europe—"in the interest of world peace."

New Yorkers, as usual, were looking for novelty and entertainment. Although located in Brooklyn, people flocked to Jack Garret's Tattoo Parlor; Jack was from London and the darling of New York's avant-garde. If you weren't in the mood for a tattoo, you could take a tour of Chinatown for a dollar, or for the same price go for a swim at the St. George's pool, which was open until midnight. The city had always lived by night, but never more than the evening of December 5, 1933, when the Late City edition of *The New York Times* broke the news: "Legal Liquor Due Tonight; City Ready to Celebrate; Liquor Stores Open Tomorrow!"

For years, people had been in favor of the repeal of Prohibition. A letter to the editor of The New York Times, written by a Dr. Henry Duncan and published in the April 12, 1930 edition stated: "People fall into one of three categories of drinkers: the millions of Americans who either do not use alcohol, or who drink so infrequently that the law does not concern them; those who are moderate in its use, and a minority, who drink to excess." According to the good doctor, these people were both a danger to themselves and to others because of their use of machinery in factories and on farms, not to mention automobiles or airplanes. Dr. Duncan was therefore in favor of some form of control for the last category of drinkers, "which has not diminished in number, and which if anything, may be larger than ever." Nevertheless, he was in favor of the repeal of the Eighteenth Amendment for the following reasons: "After ten years, it has failed to control or to stop the use of alcohol by those for whom the law was primarily intended. The law has unjustly interfered with the desires and habits of millions who use alcohol in a temperate manner." The letter ends with the following: "In case of repeal, will public opinion swing to the support of severe laws controlling the sale and use of alcohol? If not, then some day ruthlessly enforced Prohibition will come again, even to the point of war if needed, since alcohol is like a drug."

But in 1933, the "Dry Law" had been repealed, and with it, the battle of opinions and the all-absorbing topic which had divided America for more than a decade. In many of the newly-opened Manhattan bars, the event was celebrated by drinks at half-price: a cocktail for twenty-five cents, a quart of whiskey for three dollars and a bottle of imported champagne for five.

* * *

On August 2, 1934, Adolph Hitler became the Chancellor of Germany. In Vienna, the Socialists prepared to resist

the onslaught of the Nazis and their sinister projects for
"law and order." Although there was no prohibition in
Europe, the American dry laws had resulted in a wide-
spread contempt for the law. Crime became organized,
and the prisons were filled to overflow capacity.

In Manhattan, thousands of visitors flocked to the newly-
opened Planetarium for a new vision of the cosmos, while
at the same moment in Italy, Mussolini rallied 20,000
fascists for the invasion of Ethiopia. The contours of a
new world crisis were becoming visible; in Washington,
Roosevelt promised to keep America from getting "en-
tangled" in Europe's problems. Cheered on by thousands,
Mussolini prepared for war while warning the international community against interference. On December 11,
1936, the Nazis invaded the Rhineland while Hitler offered France a twenty-five year non-aggression pact. Using
the signature of a Franco-Soviet pact as a pretext, Hitler
violated the Locarno Agreement, and consequently the
Treaty of Versailles. Leaving the Throne of England to his
brother the Duke of York, Edward VIII abdicated, re-
nouncing the British crown out of love for a middle-aged
American divorcee, Wallace Simpson.

After the Wall Street crash of 1929, race relations began
to change in Manhattan—part of the slow transforma-
tion in mentalities that continued into the thirties. Black
writers of the Harlem Renaissance had already begun
looking back to their Afro-American heritage long before Malcom X, Spike Lee or other less prominent blacks
of today. Those interested in the question of race relations in New York during this period should read the

chapter entitled "Black and White Manhattan" in Anne Douglas *Terrible Honesty: Mongrel Manhattan in the 1920s*. The book explores the rejection of the prevailing lies and hypocrisy of earlier eras by a newer, younger generation of socially-committed artists, citing writers like Raymond Chandler, F. Scott Fitzgerald (*This Side of Paradise*), Eugene O'Neill, Ezra Pound (who later sympathized with the fascists), Djuna Barnes (who maintained that she never lied in her fiction) and Dashiell Hammett, all of whom were advocates of objective, hard facts concerning American life in the twenties.

In the *New Yorker Album of Cartoons* (1925-1950), published by Harpers, one cartoon in particular struck me as being perfectly representative of the thirties. The drawing depicts two well-fed capitalists in tuxedos and a sexy vamp with a long cigarette holder. In the caption, one of the men is saying to the other: "I never told her about the Depression. She would have worried."

By 1933, the financial crisis had worsened, and a nationwide bank panic occurred. The League of Nations was dissolved. Gertrude Stein touched a large public for the first time with her *Autobiography of Alice B. Toklas*, while Aldous Huxley described American life as "all movement and noise, like water gurgling out of a bath, down the drain. Yes, down the drain."

* * *

Newspapers had become big business in the twenties and even bigger in the thirties. William Randolph Hearst was the head of America's largest newspaper publishing empire, followed by the Scripps-Howard Group with twenty-six dailies. Hearst was immortalized by Orson Welles, "*l'enfant terrible du cinema*," in his classic *Citizen Kane*.

Decades earlier, from his headquarters on Park Row, the newspaper magnate Joseph Pulitzer had successfully campaigned for making the Brooklyn Bridge toll-free. Pulitzer had also launched a crusade against the great monopolies, as well as corruption in politics and the civil service. Arthur Brisbane, for whom I worked as a copy boy for more than two years, had been trained by Pulitzer before becoming Hearst's right-hand man.

In drawing upon my memories of New York for this introduction, I have been re-reading many old and not-so-old books in order to refresh souvenirs which are buried in the past. Going through the pages of H. Allen Smith's *The Life and Times of Gene Fowler*—a copy dedicated by his son Gene Jr: "For Sam, about a guy we both loved."—I came across the following anecdote in chapter 16: Walking down the streets of Manhattan one afternoon, Damon Runyon ran into Gene Fowler who had recently arrived from Denver and invited him downtown to City Hall for a memorial ceremony honoring New York's former mayor John Purroy Mitchell. Thanks to Runyon, Gene found himself standing among the visiting dignitaries, next to Teddy Roosevelt, one of his boyhood heroes. Gene had never seen Roosevelt in the flesh, but he had always associated the man with the rugged West. And there he stood, a tired overweight man, much shorter than Gene had imagined him and not at all the heroic Rough-Rider and plainsman of legend. After the ceremony, Runyon and Fowler were walking toward Park Row along the drab streets behind the World Building when a thin, dapper man approached Runyon. They chatted briefly, and Damon introduced the individual, who was none other than Senator James J. Walker. Once again, Fowler was suitably impressed, but at that time in his life he was impressed by everyone and everything in New York, including each and every cobblestone under his feet! Over dinner at Whyte's Restaurant, Runyon advised Fowler not to be so self-effacing, and cited the aphorism: "He who toots not his own horn, himself shall not be tooted." With that, he pointedly asked Gene why the hell he was wearing spats. In fact, why did he wear spats at all? Gene was by now so self-effaced that he was unable to reply.

An evening or so after, Damon took Fowler to Jack Dunstan's all-night restaurant on Sixth Avenue. Dunstan's was a watering-hole for many of the town's celebrities, and Fowler met a number of famous newspapermen, including the great Frank Ward O'Malley. Runyon also introduced Fowler to the musician Victor Herbert; after the session at Jack's, the two men taxied to the Hotel McAlpin. At the hotel entrance, Damon asked Gene to stay seated for a few minutes, since he had something important to tell him: "You can take my advice or leave it, fella," said Runyon, "but you're starting off on the wrong foot in this man's town." Runyon went on to explain how upset he was over Fowler's comments about music to Victor Herbert, not to mention the way Fowler dressed. For Runyon, Gene was behaving like "an oar out of water."

"Gene made a quick decision. The hell with New York. The hell with Arthur Brisbane and Teddy Roosevelt, and piss on Victor Herbert."

The biographer then describes how Fowler went back to Denver, but only for twenty-four hours: "New York had taken its grip on his soul, had mesmerized him." On more than one occasion, Runyon persisted in calling Fowler "a cornfield hick," but their friendship lasted a lifetime. The period in which they lived was known as the "American Intellectual Adolescence." Was it adolescence or simply modernism? Manhattan was the political, economic and cultural center of the Western world. The paradox of "terrible honesty" and Gene Fowler's "nevertheless" atmosphere of the twenties was carried over into the thirties by people like H. L. Mencken and Dorothy Parker. College students could write term-papers on the objectivity and failings of *The Age of Terrible Honesty* by taking Jean Starobinski's book *La Transparence et l'obstacle* as their model.

* * *

The "Gay" Nineties, when a tycoon like Andrew Carnegie could make 23 million dollars a year without having to pay taxes, were long gone. But in Manhattan the Ziegfeld Follies, founded in 1907, were still going strong. "The Follies" were always the most spectacular and longest-running show in Manhattan, having taken their name from the *Folies Bergere* in Paris. Ziggy's idea was to glorify the "All-American Girl": romance, adventure and a zest of sex were this great showman's stock-in-trade, especially during the Depression years. According to the March 31, 1930 issue of *Time* magazine, the new decade was inaugurated by "breadlines stretching for blocks in New York City." The Bowery YMCA was feeding 12,000 jobless people a day, while Manhattan's Church of the Transfiguration ("The Little Church around the Corner") opened free meal counters for the first time since 1907. The lines here also stretched for blocks. The demands on charity orgranizations—and for charity in general—doubled. Newspaper columnist Heywood Broun started a "Give a Job until June" crusade in the *New York Telegram*.

One of the reasons that the Depression became a world-wide phenomenon was the Hawley-Smoot Tariff of 1930 which increased the taxes on imported goods, making international trade prohibitive. An idea of the effect of the Hawley-Smoot Act on the ports of New York is given by the June 30, 1930 issue of *Time* magazine: "A dozen steamers piled on extra steam crossing the Atlantic last week, racing against time to save money. The steamer "Olympic" was a notable winner, and saved 130,000 dollars for its clients. In Manhattan, men fighting noisily in the customs-houses raced to withdraw their merchandise before the zero-hour when customs duties would be higher. Manhattan customs receipts for the day were ten times the average…". By November 3, 1930, again according to *Time*, 35,000 persons were out of work, and there was little President Hoover could do about it.

For decades, Joseph Pulitzer had campaigned against monopolies, corruption and other social evils. Like Emile Zola in France, Pulitzer had been accused of using the cause of the poor and techniques of cheap sensationalism to enrich himself. But whatever the two men's real motives, their combat for social justice would influence history and the cause of the people in the coming decades. The Norris-LaGuardia Act of 1932 gave workers the right to strong unions, while their employers were forbidden to take strikers to court. With the Wagner Act, workers won the right to collective bargaining, better working conditions and wages that have increased until the present day. The thirties were the years of the creation of unions and professional guilds. Where for example, would actors and writers be without the Writer's, Director's or Screen Actor's Guilds? Many of the same people who accused Roosevelt of being a "communist" when he created a social security system in the thirties are more than happy to cash their social security checks today. By 1937, thanks to union leaders like John L. Lewis, sit-down strikes had become an effective means for improving workers' conditions. Lead by Earl Browder, the American Communist Party created a Popular Front against world fascism, while at the same time condoning Hitler's non-aggression pact with Staline. From the ninth floor of their Manhattan office building, they doubtlessly had a different vision of "world peace."

High unemployment in the early thirties lasted until 1937. The worst year was 1933 when wages dropped, factories laid-off massively and people lived on charity, or like "Apple Annie" in Frank Capra's brilliant film *Lady for a Day*, sold fruit in the streets to survive. The breadlines were like something out of Victor Hugo's *Les Miserables*, with people crying "*du pain, du pain*" to fill their empty stomachs. The poor and the hungry gathered in Manhattan and planned a march on Washington. But instead of a revolution, America gave them cheap liquor, gambling and slot-machines. Organized crime was on the rise, and gangsters were becoming national heroes among the disenfranchised. Manhattan's most famous hoods were Jack "Legs" Diamond and "Dutch" Schultz; the latter's real name was actually Arthur Flegenheimer, a fact which never failed to amuse me.

* * *

In a *Literary Digest* dated April 12, 1930, there is a letter to the editor that begins: "Europeans may detest us, but our bewilderment over the cause is now clear. It is not due to the impending Tariff, nor the war debts, nor the League of Nations. Nor is it our love for boxing championships. Ernest Newman, the English music critic, says that the great misfortune of America and thus for Europe is—Jazz: 'If the peace of the world is to be assured, let America, for Heaven's sake, send us no more spirituals, but especially no more Jazz!'" The Englishman's attitude is in sharp contrast to the enthusiasm of the French writer Paul

Morand, who saw the potential of an American *art de vivre*: "Life," wrote Morand, "has become so harsh and brutal in Europe that I now feel like a rough pioneer myself, and like a European brute when I visit America." "Are we really so civilized?" asked Morand at an American Club of Paris banquet, and added that "Manhattan is the center of modern civilization." And this despite Lord Chesterfield, who declared a century earlier that: "For a much-travelled man, Manhattan is without the slightest interest."

* * *

If today, the Empire State Building or the twin towers of the World Trade Center are among the best-known symbols of Manhattan, the Pergola Room of the Algonquin Hotel and its famed "Round Table" was certainly a Manhattan landmark in the thirties. The artists, critics and playwrights who gathered there possessed a youthful sense of candor and criticism, and were the continuation of the spirit of "terrible honesty" of the twenties. Only now, they found themselves torn between a lingering cultural allegiance to Europe, where fascism with its simplistic but deadly philosophy of "law and order" was growing like a terrible cancer, and its direct opposite: chaotic, swinging and freedom-loving Manhattan. Europe was sinking in the disaster of bankrupt ideals, even while Manhattan witnessed the emergence of a new, mixed society which cut across social and color lines, far from Hitler's hate-filled theories

or Gobineau's concept of a "pure race." As in Dororthy
Parker's sketch, life was "An Arrangement in Black and
White." The artists and intellectuals of New York in the
thirties called themselves "The Moderns," who were lat-
er represented in the Alan Rudolph film of the same name.
Rudolph, evidently obsessed by the theme of Manhattan
in the twenties and thirties, also did a film on Dororthy
Parker. Despite the massive European exile of creative
Americans in the twenties, F. Scott Fitzgerald had already
predicted that culture and art would be centered in
Manhattan in the decades to come, rather than in
London, Vienna, Berlin or Paris.

John Keats' 1970 biography on Dorothy Parker offers another glimpse of intellectual life in Manhattan in the
thirties. Many of the Algonquin regulars found work in
the Hollywood studios, for which they harbored unlim-
ited contempt, even as they delighted in their huge salaries.
The informal gatherings in the Algonquin went all the
way back to 1919, initiated by hard-working, underpaid
writers and journalists who had a need to communicate
through literature and poetry. The phenomenon was to-
tally unique, and could only be compared to places like
the Café Procope in Paris or London's 18th-century cof-
feehouses. I had met Dorothy Parker with Robert Benchley,
her best friend and mentor, and I remember her as being
a tiny woman who asked me for my name and address. I
also recall that she wrote them on the hem of her dress,
while remarking that we were both born in the month of
August! Anita Loos, one of the other Algonquin writers
especially known for her sharp wit, remarked that

Americans were very uncultured, but many of the Algonquin regulars were a combination of eccentricity, mental aberration and pure genius similar to the European surrealists. Although it was at times fashionable to berate them among intellectuals, journalists and even old members of the group themselves, a list of the talent that gathered in the Pergola Room was quite impressive: Yascha Heifetz, Douglas Fairbanks, Harpo Marx, Edna Ferber and Herman J. Mankiewisz; earlier members included Robert Benchley, Robert Sherwood, Alexander Woolcott, Harold Ross, Donald Ogden Stewart, George S. Kaufman, Heywood Broun and Charles Mac Arthur. Many of these people were seeking fame and fortune on Broadway as actors, playwrights or producers, or on newspapers and magazines as journalists and writers, and many achieved both. Many also suffered from drinking problems or were total drunks. Needless to say, and even if several of the group's members were notorious souses, no alcohol was served on the Algonguin's premises during the Prohibition years. Dorothy Parker was supposed to have said to one of her lovers or husbands—or perhaps to each—"You don't want to be the town drunk, above all if the town in question is Manhattan." Renowned for her talent and biting wit, Parker's life ended sadly in a shabby New York hotel, despite having owned a villa in Beverly Hills, a farm in Pennsylvania and an apartment in Manhattan! The little money that remained in her estate after the sale of a Picasso was left to Martin Luther King.

* * *

Manhattan in the thirties was like a Hollywood Western: lots of shootings, crimes and murder. Reporters and journalists were highly respected—a tradition which has been carried on until the present, and which is reflected in novels, cinema and television. "Journalism," according to George Bernard Shaw," is the highest form of literature, for all the highest literature is journalism." (From *Ballyhoo, the Voice of the Press* by Silas Brent, 1927). Previously in America, newspapermen had rarely been known for their idealism or loyalty: in Thomas Jefferson's day they had been called 'turncoats' while in the thirties many were "goose-stepping" to the prevailing beat of local or national politics. But the ethics of journalism was changing: from Sinclair Lewis to H. L. Mencken, newspapermen were often talented writers or poets who expressed the human condition through a combination of facts and fiction. Being a reporter had become a thrilling adventure for both men and women. As a journalist in Manhattan, I had worked with John Huston's mother, Rhea Jaure, a tall, lean woman and crime reporter of wit and talent. John used to tease me that I had spent more time with his mother that he had. Women of Rhea's caliber—and others like her—were no longer restricted to society items or superficial news, and did the same jobs as their male colleagues with the same level of efficiency and professionalism.

"The reporter is expected to be as accurate as a chronometer, as suave as a diplomat, as callous as an insurance solicitor, as invincible as a big business go-getter," wrote Silas Brent in *Ballyhoo, the Voice of the Press*.

The illustrated tabloid press had to hook its readers and generate mass emotion, whether the story was about the death of a beloved film star such as Rudolph Valentino or a suicide, murder or simply a sports event. Sports writers had in fact become very popular and prestigious, and at times exposed the corruption behind the sports scene. Working for *The Graphic*, I wrote my first headline, announcing the death of the actress Jean Eagles—famous for her role in Somerset Maugham's play *Rain*—who had died of an overdose of drugs.

* * *

Another example of what intellectual life was like in Manhattan in the thirties can be found in the *Diary of H. L. Mencken*, published by Knopf in 1989. Mencken's biting wit made readers overlook his anti-Roosevelt stance and his alleged anti-Semitism: although he often complemented Jews for their brilliance, he was also capable of insulting them simply for being Jewish! Even though Mencken spent much of his life in Baltimore, his writings are closely linked to the cultural and intellectual activities of New York. I once learned that William Randolph Hearst had asked Mencken to replace my editor Arthur Brisbane when the latter died unexpectedly in Europe in December 1936, and that Mencken had declined the offer. In his diary, Mencken wrote about an evening at the home of Manhattan publisher Alfred Knopf where Dashiell Hammet and William Faulkner were both dead drunk and had to be carried out by a friend. In another

Samuel Fuller and Hamster Biro, the editor of the *New York Journal*

entry from his diaries—which run from 1930 to 1948—
Mencken wrote: "F. Scott Fitzgerald and his wife were
here to lunch yesterday. Mrs. Fitzgerald is a patient at the
Phibbs Clinic. The poor girl went insane in Paris a year
or so ago, and is still more or less off her base. She man-
aged to get through lunch quietly enough, but there was
a wild look in her eye, and now and then she showed
plain signs of her mental distress. Unfortunately, Fitzgerald
is a heavy drinker, and most of his experience has been
in bars...". Mencken continued his description of
Fitzgerald: "He is a charming fellow, and when sober makes
an excellent companion. Unfortunately, liquor sets him
wild and he is apt, when drunk, to knock over a dinner
table or run his automobile into a bank building."

In 1934, Mencken and Theodore Dreiser were having dinner in Manhattan; Dreiser, who had become a celebrated
author with *An American Tragedy*, boasted about being
the only American writer to receive his royalties from the
Russians in dollars: at the time, exactly five thousand a
year. Dreiser, one of the great American literary talents
of the twenties and thirties, also had an anti-Semitic
streak. He was known to have accused his publishers—
who were Jewish—of keeping two sets of books! Much
like Voltaire, Mencken was cynical and critical of everyone and everything, as can be seen in his description of
Eleanor Roosevelt addressing a WPA Workers Alliance
convention: "There was a palpable touch of patronage in
her friendliness. She spoke, not as one who has endured
the miseries of the hearers, but simply as one who has
observed them politely from afar. She was excessively

amiable, but there was something fixed and artificial in her smile. I don't think she made much impression on the poor fish before her. They cheered when she came in, and they applauded politely when she finished, but it was plain that she left them as hopeless as they were before she spoke to them…". Those were harsh words indeed for America's beloved First Lady, but then Mencken was a pure product of the period of "terrible honesty" of the twenties, described so well by Anne Douglas. What's for sure, however, is that Mencken never pulled his punches. People in the thirties were less interested in this kind of no-holds-barred honesty than in more escapist themes such as spiritualism and the possibility of life on other planets. Perhaps the popularity of the radio, combined with the apprehension of another world war, opened people to concepts such as "extra-sensory perception." The expression itself was coined by a certain Dr. Joseph B. Rhine in his best-selling book *New Frontiers of the Mind*, published in 1937. Mencken, true to his vocation of demystification and debunking, called the book "a lot of hooey" in a sardonic article of 1937, entitled "Every Man His Own Radio."

* * *

The prevailing mood of the times was given voice in Orson Welles' catastrophic *War of the Worlds* radio broadcast, which created a situation of mass panic among the listeners who believed that Welles' realistic spoof of a Martian invasion was the real thing. As Welles later admitted to Peter Bogdanovich in a taped interview, "the show was greatly popular with the public, but it was the newspapers, jealous of the power of radio, that played up the event in a negative way." (from Orson Welles and Peter Bogdanovich's *This is Orson Welles*, consisting of four cassettes of conversations between Welles and Bogdanovich spanning ten years and ten cities around the world). As Welles stated so succinctly in his conversations with Bogdanovich, "radio had become the biggest rival for newspapers." Broadcasting was taking advertising revenues away from the papers, and the press was far from happy about the situation.

The thirties were the salad days of radio in Manhattan, and as Welles remarked to Bogdanovich, there was a new show on every week. Welles' first job with ABC Network Radio was a series of broadcasts based on Victor Hugo's *Les Misérables*. His *War of the Worlds* broadcast was revelatory of the public's hunger for violence, sensationalism and escapist themes. Irony of history, Welles' sponsor for his foray into outer space was none other than the very down-to-earth Campell's Soup Company, immortalized some thirty years later in Andy Warhol's celebrated series of pop-art paintings. Decades before all this, legend has it that Horace Greely had warned Morse: "You are going to turn the newspaper industry upside-down with your invention." By the thirties, radio had become an industry in its own right, with millions of listeners tuning in to entertainment, news and advertising. The press, which had at first played up the invention of radio with great enthusiasm, now felt that radio was biting the hand that had initially nurtured it. The printed page could no longer compete with radio "air-time," which carried the actual voice of the President or famous entertainers. The impact on the public of the "little moment on the air" was enormously effective. In Manhattan, Alexander Woolcott of the Algonquin clique took to the airwaves as the "Town Crier." Radio was not only used for entertainment and advertising, but for political purposes as well. In 1937, Gerald K. Smith who had been associated with the reactionary politician Huey Long, used radio station WINS—located on 48th Street and owned by *The New York American*—to air a violent diatribe against the menace of Bolchevism and John L. Lewis, the labor leader who directed the United Mine Workers Union for more than forty years.

Publishers were so angry and frightened by the importance that radio broadcasting had taken that the president of a national broadcasting network attempted to reassure them: "There need be no fear that radio will take the place of newspapers or destroy them. There need be no fear of conflict or competition. We discuss with our clients or their advertising agencies as to whether they are advertising in the newspapers. We advise them to tie-in their newspaper and magazine advertising with the sponsorship of radio programs," reported an article in *Ballyhoo, the Voice of the Press* in 1937.

* * *

As at London's Hyde Park Corner, New Yorkers in 1937 stood on soap-boxes in Union Square to make speeches for or against communism. I often listened to these impassioned open-air debates, and I also recall my mother getting into an argument with a Bolshevik Russian poet and then inviting him home for a glass of wine.

In 1934, black-shirted American Nazis paraded in Manhattan. The sickness of the times would ultimately blossom into the anti-communist Inquisition of the fifties. Among the victims of the abominable MacCarthy era with its witchhunts, betrayals and other abject forms of human behavior were the group of actors, screenwriters and directors known as The Hollywood Ten.

Sadly enough, in the thirties most of America's Catholics were hoping for a fascist victory in Spain: Father Coughlin made anti-Roosevelt and anti-Semitic speeches and was strongly opposed to the Spanish Loyalist movement, while newspapers ran a photo of Cardinal Dougherty shaking hands with a leader of the KKK. Fortunately, the progressive social legislation proposed in 1933-34 was adopted by the government, and by 1939 America's mood had become markedly populist and pro-labor. During these years, I also remember older people reading Walter B. Pitkins' novel, *Life Begins at Forty*. The book's popularity can be explained by the consolation it offered for the wasted years of the Depression. Nevertheless, the hit song of 1935-36 was "The Music Goes 'Round and 'Round." At the same time, New York District Attorney Tom Dewey was going around Manhattan arresting racketeers, while Bruno Richard

Hauptmann went on trial for the Lindbergh kidnapping. In 1937, I saw Woolworth girls having a sit-down strike on East 14th Street, and I still remember how pretty some of them were. In 1938, a young man jumped out of a 17th-floor window at the Hotel Gotham, thereby gaining his fifteen minutes of fame with the horrified onlookers, as well as great press coverage. By the end of 1939, women's hemlines went up and Joe di Maggio —who would marry Marilyn Monroe in the fifties—was at the height of his baseball career. And even as the evil genius of Adolph Hitler clouded thinking people's minds, Charlie Chaplin wrote and directed his classic *The Great Dictator* to ridicule him.

In the course of writing this introduction to *New York in the 1930s*, I came across the following letter from the White House, signed by Franklin Delano Roosevelt: "To members of the United States Expeditionary Forces. You are a soldier of the United States Army, and you have embarked for distant places where the war is being fought. Upon the outcome depends the freedom of your lives, the freedom of the lives of those you love, your fellow-citizens and your people. Never were the enemies of freedom more tyrannical, more arrogant, more brutal…". The President's letter goes on to exhort the soldiers to fight against Hitler and his allies.

I was one of the survivors of Omaha Beach, and lucky enough to still be here to remember the *inoubliables souvenirs* of Manhattan in the thirties—the "Big Bottle," as Hemingway called it. Filmmakers like Woody Allen can't seem to leave Manhattan these days, but to get the feeling of what the city was like in the twenties and thirties, let's look at the last chapter of Gene Fowler's *Skyline*:

"I listened to the older men in the inns and bars, their voices in the wind. Of course, there is one comforting thought; had you listened to sound advice, you would have avoided some of your most valuable mistakes. It takes a bit of do-it-yourself philosophy to keep from growing sad or lonely. For example, when you see what has happened to the Camelot you once knew, the Island of Manhattan.

Or dying on the installment plan whenever an old friend's name appears in the obituary pages of the *Times*. Not only has the City changed in fact, but more important to you, in fancy. Your reason tells you that young men and women are this moment finding it, as you once did, a region of magic, a city of dreams and singing stones. But with all its vaunt of size and importance and furies of voice, it makes you suddenly a stranger. Old symbols have been taken from the shrines. The mellowed brownstones are gone. The old nooks, the venerable inns, the lovely gloom of Park Row, Perry's Alcoholic Drugstore, Dr. de Garmo's Chestnut Oven, the flophouse where kidnapper Pat Crowe snored through his binges and the monstrous Post Office building at the southern tip of the tongue of City Hall Park—a thousand and seventy places you knew, and where you walked day upon day in the wind. Blow, winds of yesterday! Blow across the stripped sands where the grassy dunes once dared to rise. Sing a wild song of remembrance at the place of the lost dunes, where youth once stood looking out upon the sea—'Till Kingdom Come."

If I end here with Gene Fowler's words, it is because he and so many other artists of the past and present have proven that the electric wonders of 42nd Street and Broadway or the skyscrapers of Manhattan can still inspire a sense of mystery and poetry. But another comment he once made about Manhattan still rings just as true across the decades: "Manhattan seldom wants you, but you'll always want Manhattan!"

The New York Waterfront

The southern tip of Manhattan in the late 1930s

Above and *opposite page:* Battery Park and the financial district

Above: Ellis Island, the former U.S. Immigration Center.
Opposite page: Manhattan seen from the Saint George Hotel in Brooklyn

Immigrants arriving on Ellis Island, 1939

Landing formalities, Ellis Island

A ship off Liberty Island

Excursion boat from Manhattan to Liberty Island

Coney Island Beach, Brooklyn

Coney Island Beach, 1936

Luna Park at Coney Island

Side-show posters at Luna Park

Side-show attractions at Coney Island

The Merry-Go-'Round at Coney Island

The Manhattan docks on the Hudson River

Above: The East River docks.
Opposite page: Battery Park

Ferry terminal near Battery Park

Manhattan skyline from the Brooklyn docks

Southern Manhattan: Ferry terminal on the Hudson River with the Woolworth
Building in the background

Ferry leaving Manhattan. In the background, the Bank of Manhattan Building

Downtown

Brooklyn Bridge from the Municipal Building

Brooklyn Bridge

South Street from the Manhattan Bridge

Brooklyn Bridge and the Manhattan skyline

Lower Manhattan and the East River

The Bank of Manhattan Building and the East River

Battery Park and the New York Aquarium (now the Clinton National Monument)
on the waterfront

Battery Park under the snow

Above: George Washington's statue on the steps of the Treasury Building
(now the Federal Hall National Memorial) on Wall Street.
Opposite page: Wall Street

Demonstration in front of the Treasury Building the day after the stock market crash of 1929

Demonstrators during the financial crisis of 1929

Strikers in the streets of Manhattan around 1938

A striker in 1930

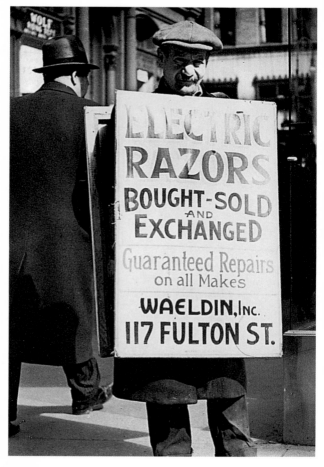

Man with a sandwich-board advertisement on Fulton Street

A Manhattan mailman

Selling pretzels on a city street-corner

A cookie cart

The Fulton Street Market

Fulton Street

The East River Docks

The South Street Fish Market, near Fulton Street

Manhattan's City Hall, seen from Chatham Square, 1938

City Hall with the Brooklyn Bridge in the background

Mafia kingpin Lucky Luciano entering the Supreme Court Building in 1938

Fiorello Laguardia, the mayor of New York from 1933 to 1945

Above: Fiorello Laguardia destroying slot-machines.
Opposite page: Selling roasted chic-peas on First Avenue

Girls carrying boxes of matzos for Passover, Columbia Street, 1933

A goat and a passer-by on Coenties Slip

Greenwich Street, Tribeca

Fourth Avenue and 12th Street

A market in lower Manhattan between 8th and 13th Street

A street market on the lower-west side of Manhattan

Washington Square Arch and Park

Saint Vincent's Clinic (now Saint Vincent's Hospital),
Seventh Avenue and 11th Street

60 GRAMERCY PARK WEST

Above: Roosevelt and his grand-daughter Anna Curtis Dall
in front of his Manhattan residence on 20th Street near Gramercy Park.
Opposite page: The Gramercy Park Hotel, Lexington Avenue and 21st Street

29th Street between Lexington and Third Avenue

28th Street

Midtown

Above: A newspaper stand on Fifth Avenue near the Flatiron Building.
Preceding page: Penn Station, Seventh Avenue between 31st and 33rd Street

Above: Madison Square and the New York Life Insurance Building seen from
the Flatiron Building.
Opposite page: The main hall of Pennsylvania Station

Demolition of the Sixth Avenue elevated line at 35th Street

Sixth Avenue and the elevated line

Subway passengers

Subway passengers on the Sixth Avenue line

City officials inspecting a subway car, 1933

The interior of a subway car

Macy's department store on Seventh Avenue between 34th and 35th Street

The Empire State Building under construction in the early 1930s.
The building was completed in 1931

Above: The lobby of the Empire State Building.
Opposite page: The Empire State Building with the Chrysler Building
in the background, seen from the Port Authority Bus Terminal, 1933

Fifth Avenue

Easter Parade on Fifth Avenue

Above: Main entrance of the New York Public Library,
Fifth Avenue and 42nd Street.
Opposite page: The rear of the New York Public Library and Bryant Park

Times Square in 1932

The Ziegfeld Follies Theater, Times Square

Theaters on 49th Street, off Broadway

The Chick Webb Band, 1931

Frank Sinatra (right) with three other members of the Hoboken band:
Frank Tamburro, Jimmy Petro and Patty Prince

Times Square around 1933

The Paramount Theater on Broadway near Times Square

Theater marquee announcing the Benny Goodman Orchestra and Frank Sinatra

Astor Theater marquee advertising the film *Queen Christine* with Greta Garbo

The Times Square theater district

Theaters on Seventh Avenue and 49th Street, around 1933

Above: Grand Central Station seen from Park Avenue, around 1936.
Opposite page: Access ramp to Grand Central Station on 42nd Street, around 1940

Grand Central Station, around 1938

Above and *following page:* The main hall of Grand Central Station

Above: The International Flower Show at Grand Central Station.
Following page: The Chrysler Building under construction.
The building was completed in 1930

RCA. Building at the Rockefeller Center

Radio City Music Hall, the largest theater in the world. This theater opened in 1932

Above: Sak's Fifth Avenue department store, on Fifth Avenue and 49th Street.
Opposite page: The RCA Building, Rockefeller Center, 1938

The Roosevelt Hotel, Madison Avenue and 45th Street

The Gotham Hotel (now Hotel Maxim's of Paris), Fifth Avenue and 55th Street

Fifth Avenue and 53rd Street, around 1937

Fifth Avenue and 46th Street, around 1933

A view of Fifth Avenue to the south

Skyscrapers

The New York Central Building (now the Helmsley Building)
on Park Avenue

A view of Park Avenue to the north, around 1935

Above: The Waldorf Astoria Hotel, Park Avenue and 50th Street.
Opposite page: The entrance to the Waldorf Astoria Hotel on Park Avenue

Central Park
and Uptown

Columbus Circle, Broadway and Eighth Avenue

The Hotel Pierre on Fifth Avenue and 61st Street, facing Central Park

Above: The Plaza Hotel on Fifth Avenue and 59th Street, facing Central Park.
Opposite page: Central Park

The Hotel Pierre (left) and the Plaza Hotel at the foot of Central Park

A view of Central Park to the south

New york in the 1930s

South east corner of Central Park

The Planetarium, Central Park West between 77th and 81st Street

Ice-skating at Wollman Rink in Central Park

Central Park under the snow

West 125th Street in Harlem

The Big Apple Jazz club on Seventh Avenue in Harlem, 1932

Above: Ella Fitzgerald with drummer Chick Webb's band at the Ashbury Park Casino, 1938.
Opposite page: Billie Holiday at the Big Apple in 1936

The Cotton Club, 48th Street and Broadway, 1938

Duke Ellington (with saxophone), O. Hardwicke, H. Carney,
H. Bigar and T. Hodges at the Cotton Club in 1932

Cab Calloway performing at the Cotton Club in 1935

Lionel Hampton playing the xylophone

The Duke Ellington Band

Above: Traffic leaving the Triborough Bridge in Harlem, around 1936.
Opposite page: Traffic to New Jersey on the George Washington Bridge,
opening day, 1931

Reference Works

Anne Douglas, *Terrible Honesty: Mongrel Manhattan in the 1920s,* Farrar Straus & Giroux, 1995

Lorenz Lee, *The Art of the New Yorker: 1925-1995,* Knopf, 1995

Gertrude Stein, *The Autobiography of Alice B. Toklas,* Penguin Books, 1989

Gene Fowler, *Skyline,* Viking Press, 1961

Harry Allen Smith, *The Life and Legend of Gene Fowler,* William Morrow & Co, 1977

Dorothy Parker, "Arrangement in Black and White" in *The Collected Dorothy Parker*, Penguin Books, 1973

John Keats, *You Might As Well Live: The Life and Times of Dorothy Parker,* Simon and Schuster, 1970

H.L. Mencken, *Feche Diary of H.L. Mencken,* Knopf, 1989

Theodore Dreiser, *An American Tragedy,* Ty Crowell Co, 1972

Joseph Banks Rhine, *New Frontiers of the Mind: The Story of the Duke Experiments,* Greenwood Publishing Group, 1972

Silas Bent, *Ballyhoo, the Voice of the Press,* Boni and Liveright, 1927

POCKET 𝓟 ARCHIVES
HAZAN